I Gave My Mom a Castle

POEMS BY JEAN LITTLE

ILLUSTRATIONS BY KADY MACDONALD DENTON

ORCA BOOK PUBLISHERS

To my sisters-in-law, Pat and Donna, with my thanks for
all they have given me over the years.

JL

Text copyright © 2003 Jean Little
Illustrations copyright © 2003 Kady MacDonald Denton

National Library of Canada Cataloguing in Publication Data
Little, Jean, 1932-

I gave my mom a castle / Jean Little.

ISBN 1-55143-253-6

1. Children's poetry, Canadian (English)* 2. Gifts--Juvenile poetry. I. Title.

PS8523.I77I28 2003   jC811'.54   C2003-910733-7

PR9199.4.L555I28 2003

First published in the United States, 2003

Library of Congress Control Number: 2003106254

Summary: A collection of prose poems, mini stories about the joys and pains of giving and
receiving, featuring a wide cast of characters from toddlers to teens.

Teachers' guide available from Orca Book Publishers.

Orca Book Publishers gratefully acknowledges the support of its publishing programs
provided by the following agencies:
the Department of Canadian Heritage, the Canada Council for the Arts, and the British
Columbia Arts Council.

Design by Christine Toller
Printed and bound in Canada

Orca Book Publishers
1030 North Park Street
Victoria, BC Canada
V8T 1C6

Orca Book Publishers
PO Box 468
Custer, WA   USA
98240-0468

06 05 04 • 5 4 3 2

Contents

Introduction

Where did this book come from?

I think this book began with a sweater and skirt my Aunt Gretta knitted for me when I was in Grade Five. She must have worked very hard on it. It was a blue ribbed skirt sewn onto a sleeveless cotton top with a pink-and-blue sweater to wear over the vest part. I loathed it! Nobody else in Miss Marr's class had a suit anything like it. My mother was furious at me for not seeing how much love and labor had gone into its making. It fit me. I had to wear it no matter what, and I discovered that not every gift is welcome.

My sister Pat wore it when I grew too big for it. She was not keen on it either. I hope Aunt Gretta never guessed.

I loved getting presents, though. Other people's parents brought them gifts when they came home from trips. Ours didn't. I would sit at the window watching for the car just in case they changed their minds. They never did.

One Christmas when I was a teenager, we decided we should draw names and give one present each. My brother Hugh and I drew each other. He bought me an expensive Liberty scarf. I got him a subscription to *The New Yorker*. We pretended to be thrilled, but we were both deeply disappointed. We had tried so hard to be grown up, but really we were not. We both wanted good books to read.

These experiences, and many more, got me interested in the art of giving. There was the wonderful day Aunt Gretta bought me roller skates on my little sister's birthday. She also bought me a puppy once. He was on sale for one dollar at the market. She was such a foolish but understanding aunt.

Like all children, I longed for mail. Adults got parcels and fistfuls of letters. I got none. Then a friend of Mother's sent me a nightgown in the mail with a card reading, "Happy Unbirthday, Jeanie!" I loved getting a totally unexpected present.

I could make a list of gifts: the quilt my sister made me of "a partridge in a pear tree"; all the Anne books from Mother the year I turned thirty-five (the last one was away down under the covers so I hit my foot on it when I got into bed); Susie, my West Highland white terrier, from Mother when I came home to live after university; a locket with butterfly wings in it from an elderly lady who liked my poems when I was fifteen; a chocolate cake and balloons brought to my hospital room when the first copy of *Mine for Keeps* was delivered to my bedside – all lovely, all memorable.

I have grown to love choosing the perfect gift for a friend – and in my books, the characters are forever giving wonderful gifts.

My very favorite, perhaps, was words spoken by my mother just before her death. I was listening through a nursery monitor and heard the doctor say, "It must be so hard for you, growing confused and being in such pain, Flora."

Mother replied quietly, "It would be hard – except that Jean is always here." I cried and cried and felt cherished and rewarded.

So I began writing poems about gifts – and this book is the result. I hope it is a gift you enjoy. Each of Kady MacDonald Denton's illustrations is a rich and lovely present to me. Thank you, Kady. And my niece Maggie's faith in the poems is a present I treasure too.

Velvet

"I want a dog for my birthday," I told Mom.
"Put it on your list," she said.
"I don't want anything else. Just a dog.
And I really will take care of him."

I told her exactly what kind of dog, too.
I wanted a big dog, a golden retriever
Or a Lab.
I wanted one with soft ears and big eyes.
I wanted a dog to run beside me through the fields.
I wanted one with a long waggy tail.
I dreamed he'd follow me everywhere and
Sleep on my bed.
I decided to call him Skip…or maybe Shadow.

I got a dog.

Mom picked her out.
Her name is Velvet.
She's a pug.
She's as black as coal.
Her tail is short and curly.
She can run, but not across fields.
She snuffles and snorts.

My dad says she's the ugliest little brute
He's ever laid eyes on.
"That's no dog for a boy," he told my mother.

He's wrong.
Velvet adores me.
She is perfect.

The Bulb

I am the fourth daughter in my family.
They kept trying for a boy.
Since I was born on my gran's birthday,
They asked her to name me.
I used to wish they hadn't.

Most people call me Mary,
And I never used to correct them.

When Gran turned ninety and I turned nine,
She sent me a mysterious box.
It had nothing written on it, and inside it
Was this big brown ugly bulb.
Mother gave me the letter that had come with it.
"This is you," it said.
"Follow the instructions below and
You will see yourself growing up into a woman."

I was kind of mad, if you want to know.
What a terrible present!
But Mom made sure I did what Gran said.
Nothing happened for ages.

Then out of the top, which stuck out of the dirt,
Sprouted a fat green shoot.
I guessed that must be me starting to grow.
Then I turned into a tall, gangly teenager.
I kind of got interested.
There were lots of buds.

Finally, overnight almost,
The thing burst into enormous flowers.
They glowed.
I've never seen anything like them.
Wow!

Now I correct people sometimes.
"My name's not really Mary," I say.
"It's Amaryllis."

Anywhere You Like

I was the only kid at home this Christmas.
My parents asked me to be polite and I was.
It was not easy.
People kept patting me.
On Boxing Day, they smiled at me.
"You were so good all day," they said,
"That we've decided to let you choose.
We'll go anywhere you like."
"Anywhere?" I said.
"Anywhere," they said.
"Promise?" I said.
"We promise," they said.
"Disney World," I said.

I knew they didn't mean it.
We went to Pizza Hut.

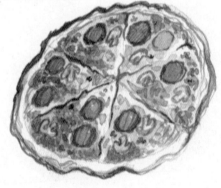

My Mother Got Me

My mother gave me a china doll
Like one she wanted when she was small.

I'd told her I wanted Dentist Barbie.

My mother gave me a string of pearls
Like her sisters got when they were girls.

I'd told her I wanted dangling earrings.

In a secondhand bookshop, my mother found
Little Women, leather bound.

I'd asked for the latest Babysitters' Club.

All I can say is
I'm glad I've got Grandma.
She has trouble hearing sometimes
But no trouble listening.

The Tree

Matthew Bluesky was the smallest kid in his class.

When he was in Grade Two,
His school planted five tiny trees out in front.
"They will grow quickly," his teacher said.
"By the time you are in Grade Five,
They will be taller than I am."

The tree Matthew helped plant was the smallest.
He watched carefully, but he did not see it grow at all.
When nobody was looking,
Matthew would sidle over to it.
"Grow, little tree, grow," he would whisper.
"You can do it."

In May, the Bluesky family moved to Edmonton,
So Matthew had no chance to see what happened next.
After a while, he forgot to wonder.

When he was twenty, Matthew rode past his old school.
He stopped his motorbike and stared.
The five trees were taller than the school.
He went closer to be sure.
It was true.
His tree stood tallest of all.

This time, Matthew Bluesky did not whisper.
"Way to go, tree," he yelled.

Some little kids were going in from recess.
One extra-short girl stopped.
She looked away up to Matthew's face.
"Are you a giant?" she asked solemnly.
"I used to be shorter than you," said Matthew.
"I was a runt.
Give yourself time, kid."

My Young Legs

"Danny," says my mother, "you have young legs.
Would you run upstairs and get my car keys for me?
I left them on my bedside table.
Hurry, darling. I'm already late."

I get the keys.
They are in the bathroom on the windowsill.

"Run out to the mailbox and fetch the paper, Dan.
I know it's Nelson's job,
But his bus came early," my dad says.
"Some fresh air will do you good."

I fetch him his paper.
He barely glances at the headlines,
Gulps down his coffee and drives off to work.

"Drat. I left my ball of green yarn in my room," Gran says.
"Could you be a dear, Daniel, and bring it to me?
You can be up and back
While I'd still be getting out of this chair."

I bring it. I go back later for the blue yarn
And a different set of knitting needles.
She's out of her chair, talking on the phone.
I'm almost late for school.

"Daniel T., take this envelope
Down to the principal's office for me.
He's in a hurry for it so don't dawdle," says Mr. Krantz.

I take it. I have to wait to bring something back.

I miss half of my French period.

On and on I run, all day long, on my speedy young legs.
I am not once rude but I do get tired.
Just before supper
I flop down flat on the living room carpet
And shut my eyes.

"What's the matter, Dan?" my father says.

"It's my young legs. They're wearing out.
I am exhausted," I moan.

"Nonsense," he says.
"You do nothing but loaf around all day.
After supper you should go out and run a few lengths of
The lane to keep yourself in shape."

"No," I say politely.
"I have homework to do.
I am writing a report on child labor."

I do it — sitting down.

The Summer Cottage

We have a summer cottage.
In February or March,
When school is too much
And the world is covered with slush,
I sit and dream about it.

Going out in the old rowboat,
Which my mother calls the Polly Wolly Doodle,
And exploring the islands too small to build on.

Playing Hearts and passing the Dirty Dorry
To my father — or whoever is winning.

Lying in bed listening to the squirrels
Playing tag on the roof.

Canoeing up the road of silver
The moon lays across the still lake.

You have time to read there
And there are lots of old books
From years back,
Good ones like Prydain Chronicles
Or *The Dark Is Rising*.
I read all of those at the cottage
And I always reread them there.

It is like I think heaven ought to be.
It has a woodsy smell
And the spooky laughter of loons.
They are there every summer.

I can't imagine not going there.
I am nearly fourteen and I've gone there
Every summer since I was born.

But on our first night at the cottage this summer
I heard my mom say to my dad,
"It's getting to be too much,
Keeping up this place.
Soon the kids will be too old for it.
Maybe we should think about selling, Dave.
It needs a lot of work done on it.
A new septic system and the roof fixed.
And I really would like to stay home and

Jean Little

Work in my own garden some summer."

One of my sisters is seventeen
And she acts too old to live.
But the other one is only ten.

I could hardly breathe.
Dad came here when he was a kid,
And they spent their honeymoon
Right in this old cottage.
Mom's family rented a place across the lake
And Mom met Dad at the store in Windermere.
She persuaded her folks to come back the next year.
She got a job at one of the hotels on Lake Rosseau
So she could keep coming over.
They got engaged on our dock.
They've told us over and over.

"No, Margie.
Not yet," Dad said.

"The kids are nowhere near too old.
I'm not too old either.
You ARE aging, I know,
So you can stay home if you like.
We might manage on our own.
I don't know how, but…"

There was this funny silence.

I crept close and craned my neck to see
What they were up to.

He was kissing her.
And she was not fighting him off.
Wow!

That seems to have settled things for now.
But…
Oh, please, don't let her think about selling.
How could I live through the winter?

Besides, the chipmunks come up on the porch
And eat out of our hands.
We couldn't let them starve,
Not innocent little chippies.

My Brother's Laugh

My little brother has an incredible laugh.
When he lets it loose, you can't help laughing back.
He really cracks you up.
If I could bottle his laugh,
I'd send it to all the sad people in the world.
For a few seconds at least, everyone would be happy.

The Parrot Speaks

Our parrot, Henry Higgins, talks a blue streak.
He screams like my sister and whines and says mean things.
"Quit that, you little brat!" he shouts in her voice.
"You shut up," he hollers.
"Not fair," he yells. "Not fair."

Yesterday, when we were having a friendly fight,
Mom dragged us into the room across the hall from Henry
And made us sit and listen to him.
He doesn't say a word if you are standing next to his cage.

"This is how you sound," she told us.
"Listen to yourselves."

She went to peel potatoes, but she kept an eye on us.

"Let's teach him a new word," I whispered to my sister.
We began working on it then and there,
Although we could not agree on just one word.
We repeated the new words to him for about a week
When Mom wasn't listening.

Today he did it at last.
She heard him say, "What great kids!"
And then, looking straight at Mom, he said,
"Rachel, you are a big idiot."

The crazy thing is, although she pretended she was mad,
I heard her bragging about it over the phone.

As if we had done her a favor.

What great kids!

Stand-In

I was the stand-in three years in a row.
Mariella Hodge's costumes were just my size.
She had acting talent.
I had dreams of glory.

I prayed and prayed
That she would get deathly ill for just one night
And I could get to star.

God listened.
Maybe.

She got some flu bug that made her throw up
Every five minutes, all night long.

I was helped into her dress.
I knew the lines.
I was shoved on stage.
It was my big moment.

And I could not do it.
I froze solid.
My tongue felt like thick dusty felt.

I heard Mr. Jessup moan,
"We don't have a stand-in for the stand-in.
Pull yourself together, June."

I gulped and squeezed out the first line.
I hoped I would improve, but I didn't.

They gave me a sympathy clap.
Mr. Jessup hugged me.
"You are a brick, June," he said.

I did not tell him but
It is no fun being a brick.

Taking Time

I heard Mom talking to her friend Asmina.
She was telling her what she thought
Of the latest Dick Francis book.

"Oh, you are so lucky," Asmina said.
"I'm run right off my feet these days.
I wish I had time to read."

"You have exactly the same amount of time
As the rest of us," Mom said.
"Twenty-four hours a day.
One lifetime, in fact.
You just choose to use it in other ways."

Asmina sounded shocked.
"You don't understand," she began.

"Yes, I do." Mom laughed.
"You work long hours at your office.
You play bridge and golf
And you go to that gourmet cooking class.
There's nothing wrong with your choices.
But you could choose to read instead.
It matters to me to read,
So I take time for it."

"Dick Francis?" Asmina said in a teasing voice.
"Sure," my mother shot back.
"I'm saving *War and Peace* until I break my leg."

I liked what she said.

So today, when she sent me to clean up my room,
I made my choice.
I began to reread my Harry Potter books.
After all, I only have one lifetime.

I wish I had time to be tidy,
But I do not.

The Birthday Message

John ran away from home when he was sixteen.
He couldn't take it any longer.
His father was always yelling at him
And his mother seemed to do nothing but whine.
"If only you'd be polite to him, John..."
"If only you'd try harder, John..."
"If only you'd clean up after yourself, John..."
"If only I'd stayed single..."

It was this last one that finally got to him.
If she'd stayed single, where would he be?
Nowhere.

He planned his going, saved up for it.
He left in summer, so if worse came to worst
And he had to sleep out, he wouldn't freeze.
But he got a job at a fast-food place
On the other side of the city.
It was the run-down side where his dad never came.

Then August arrived.
His birthday was on the 3rd.
He waited till he knew they'd both be at church.
Then he phoned home.
"You have reached the Brown house. We are out.
Leave a message after the beep," his dad's voice rasped.

John swallowed and then spoke very clearly.
"Hey, Mom," he said, "I'm okay.
Thanks for having me."
He almost hung up. Then he spoke once more.
"I'll be seeing you," he said.

The First Dandelion

Our baby got all excited this morning.
"Me got you a pwesent," he said.
Then, very solemnly, he handed me a
Drooping, raggedy yellow flower.

I looked at it and then at his proud expression.

"It's the fust dandelion," he told me.

I was going to educate him — and then
I thanked him instead.

It was a buttercup really.
Not a dandelion, that was for sure.

But he is just two and a half.
Manners matter more than botany at that age.
And he had chosen me.

Moon Dance

Every night, his mother read him *Goodnight Moon*.
She read it to him before he was born.
She told him so.
She read him other books too,
But the last one, just before she kissed him and went away,
Was always *Goodnight Moon*.
When there was a moon, she held him up to see it.
"Moon. See the moon," she crooned.
"It's saying 'Good night' to you.
Good night, moon."

"Night, moon," he learned to say.
It always made his mother smile.

He liked his firetruck book better,
But he did not tell her.
He knew *Goodnight Moon* was her favorite.

Then, one night, he woke up.
His mother was gone.
The whole house was asleep.
And the moon was looking in his window.

He stared up at her and smiled.

"Night, moon," he said.

The moon leaned closer
And laid a square of silver light
Down on his bedroom floor.

He looked at it for a long time.
He put his sleeper feet over the edge of his new bed,
Slid to the floor
And stepped onto the carpet of silver light.

Then he danced a slow, careful dance.

The moon grew very bright indeed.

He heard her whisper to him.
"Good night, boy," she said.
He remembered in the morning, but he did not tell.

It was their secret, his and the moon's.

Family Pig

My uncle Max is a pig.
He eats like a pig.
He snuffles and snorts
And shoves in bites bigger than mouthfuls.
He is disgusting.
And he complains about my mother's cooking.

"Too spicy," he grumbles, passing his plate for seconds.
"But I'll do my bit
So you won't have to eat it again tomorrow."

He comes without being invited.

I don't know why they let him in.

Last night he did it once too often,
And I saw my mother blink back tears.

"Stop it, Uncle Max," I yelled at him.
"If you have to eat like a pig,
Do it somewhere else
And stop insulting my mother!"

They sent me to my room.

My sister told me later that
Our uncle went blotchy purple
And marched out the door,
Slamming it behind him.

"I never heard the like," he bellowed.
"I won't be back until that boy apologizes."

I got told off, of course.
"He was our guest," Dad said.

But nobody has mentioned apologizing.

Valentines

When Valentine's Day comes,
You have to give everyone a card
Or nobody.
Some mothers bring cupcakes all around.

One day, my mother was telling us
How it was in the Olden Days.
When she was a kid, they had this decorated box,
And the teacher called out the names.
You put in cards for people you liked.
But you never signed them.

She gave a boy she liked a card that said,
"Will you be my knight in shining armor?"

"I could never have done it
If I had had to sign it," she said.
"He showed it to his friends and smirked.
I changed my mind about him in less than a week."

"But what if nobody put one
In the box for you?" I asked her.

"That never, ever happened," she said slowly.
"Well, only once.
There was a new girl who was mean as dirt.
She was a bully and a tattletale.
But I remember sitting there
Watching the piles of cards on the desks.
They were all growing, some slowly
And others so fast the cards fell onto the floor.
Except for Rachel's.

Rachel just sat looking out the window
And keeping her face stiff.
Finally, she did get one."

"Thank goodness," I said.
Just hearing about it made me feel sick.

Mother was silent for a moment.
Then she said, in a low voice,
"It was from the teacher.
She put in one for each of us."

"That is horrible," I said.

"I agree," said my mother.
"We must have all felt that way
Because the next year she got quite a few,
Even though she was still not one bit nice."

"Did you give her one?" I asked.

Mother looked at me.

"What do you think?" she said.

"I think you gave her one," I said.

"I gave her two — just in case," Mother said.

I hugged her.

And on Valentine's Day, I gave her two
In memory of the Olden Days.

The Melon

One afternoon in early summer,
Joanna was wandering around the garden
And came upon a small watermelon.
It was growing by itself on a piece of vine
Which had headed away from the rest.

Joanna squatted down and
Stroked it with one finger.
She undid the safety pin that
Was holding the zipper on her jeans closed.
Very carefully, she used the point as a pen
And wrote one word on the small fruit.

Then she forgot all about it.

One evening in late summer,
Mom told Joanna's little brother
To stay on his chair.
"We are having a mystery dessert," she said.

She left the room and returned with a large melon.
While they watched,
She turned it in her hands.
On the side, in large clear letters, was one word.
ZACHARY.

Joanna's brother's eyes grew wide.
"That's my name," he said.
"Yes," said their mother.
"But you can't write your name.
Who do you think wrote it on this mystery melon?"

Joanna bit her lips and lowered her eyes.
But Zachary was not looking at her.

"Mother Nature?" he said in hushed tones.

No Book

Every year since I was born,
They've given me a book for Christmas.
Some have been babyish.
Some have been too hard.
Some have been absolutely perfect.
But always a book.

Until this year.

I never knew Christmas afternoon
Could be so long.

Making Friends With Rosie

There's a girl in my class I want to make friends with.
When something is funny, the two of us smile
At exactly the same moment.
I like her already.
She came a week ago
But I haven't spoken to her yet.
I'll do it though —
As soon as I figure out how to begin.
It is tricky because she is blind.
Everybody else is fussing over her.
"I'll help you, Rosie," they coo.
They tell her stuff she doesn't want to know
And they grab her elbow and push her around
As though she's a walking doll
Or a puzzle piece.
They ask her dumb questions like
"How do you get dressed?" and
"What do you think colors look like?"

I want her to know right away
That her blindness is not what I like about her.
It's her laugh I like
And the things she says.
She's reading *Izzy Willy Nilly* on tape.
I love that book.
Maybe I could start with that.

Loving an Elf

My sister's name is Millicent
But my parents used to call her Elf.
It did fit her.

When she was five and small for her age,
Her eyes were greeny gray.
Her hair was the reddish brown of peeled conkers.
She had this crooked little grin.

I am four years older.
My hair is plain brown.
My eyes are brown too.
Good ordinary brown.
My smile is fine...not impish.
When I walk, I walk.

The elf danced.

But I did love her.
I still do.
Everybody does.

Back then, when she was five and I was nine,
She fell asleep when I was pushing her on the swing.
I didn't notice.
Well, I had things on my mind.
The elf slipped off when the swing was
At the top of its sweep.
She crashed down with one leg bent under her
And broke it.
Badly.
It was terrible.

She didn't even scream.
She just lay there, white under her freckles,
And looked at me as though I were a stranger.

She had to go to the hospital.
They operated.
Then she lay in a high bed in traction.

She acted just like herself,
But they kept saying how brave she was.

All the aunts and uncles and grandparents
Plus her kindergarten teacher
Plus the lady next door
Plus our babysitter
Went to see her
And took her presents.

"She looks so small," Mom said,
"With her leg in that awful contraption."

"How could you not have noticed?"
My father asked me again and again.

Then, one morning, she came home.
An orderly carried her to the car.
Behind him marched two nurses.
They were bearing the piled-up presents.

I stared at her through the car window.

And I hated her.
I could not help myself.

Loving an elf non-stop is impossible
When your name is Jane
And all they ever call you is
Jane.

I forgive myself.

Now I am sixteen and she is twelve.
She is a pain.
She is almost fat.
Sulky too.

I have no trouble loving her
Now she is not elfish.
I tell my parents to be patient with her.

They are doing their best.

Mrs. Hanover

Our school principal, Mrs. Hanover,
Calls the boys "dear" and the girls "hon" or "sweetie."
My mother thinks it's lovely.
"You can tell she's fond of children," she says.
We know better.
She just can't be bothered to learn our names.

The Fishing Rod

"Your father really loves you," Ma said.
"You should get him something special for his birthday."
I got him a fishing rod.
Uncle Willie told me which one was worth buying.
It took every cent I had.
"I'd like us to go fishing together,"
I wrote on the card.

He ripped off the paper and glanced at the rod.
"If you want to fish, ask your Uncle Willie.
He's got time to waste," he growled.
"I'm too busy working to pay the bills around here."

The next day was Saturday.
Pa spent all afternoon in front of the TV
Watching the double-header at the Dome.

When his next birthday comes,
I'm getting him a tie,
The cheapest tie I can find.

Pa hates ties.

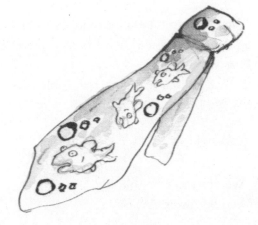

How I Got Adopted

"They said we were going to adopt a baby,"
My big brother said.
"A sweet little baby to be my sister."

I giggled.
"Then what?" I said.

"There weren't any sweet little babies,
So they said they would take a big baby.
She'd be more fun for me anyway,"
My big brother said.

"Then what?" I asked.

"There weren't any big babies.
Not one.
So they said we'd get a nice toddler,
One who could play with me a bit,"
My big brother said.

"Then what?" I asked him, bouncing up and down.

"There weren't any nice toddlers to be had.
So they finally said they'd take a rotten kid
Nobody wanted,
A great nuisance, a pest, a horrible brat,"
My big brother said.

"And then..."

"We got you," he told me.
"And you were AWFUL."

"But you wanted me, didn't you?" I said,
Throwing myself on his lap.

"Right," he said, pushing me off.
"Somebody had to take you, after all."

"How about now?" I asked him, knowing what he'd say.

"Now I could not live without you,
My darling sister," he teased.
Then we had a wrestling fight
With him only using one arm.

But he meant it.
I know because
I couldn't live without him either.

Two Dogs Waiting

I'll comfort you with apples
Or an upstairs maid,
A plum tree, a ball gown
Stiff with brocade.

Tell me of the treasure
You cannot resist.
Would you like a nugget
As big as your fist?

A doll's house? A tea rose?
A carriage and four?
A genuine horseshoe
To hang above your door?

I'll make you a melody
Upon my guitar.
I'll give you a skipping rope,
I'll steal you a star.

Champagne or cider?
A mountain? A sea?
A week in Spain? An airplane?
A cup of hot tea?

I will give you castles,
Or Chippendale chairs,
Or two dogs waiting
At the top of the stairs.

Keep the maid, the apples,
The star you stole for me,
The rose and the nugget,
The song and the sea.

Keep the gown, the doll's house,
The carriage and four,
And you may hang the horseshoe
Above your own door.

I couldn't cope with castles.
The mountain you may keep.
The former would be drafty,
The latter too steep.

Keep the rope for skipping,
And the white plum tree,
The champagne, the cider,
The trip to Spain, the tea.

Even keep the airplane
And the antique chairs,
But leave me the two dogs
Waiting on the stairs.

The Good Example

I'm sick of setting a good example.
I'm sick of pretending I like cabbage.
I'm sick of always letting him have the bigger piece.
I'm sick of not biting my nails.
I'm fed up with pretending to be brave about storms.
"Your sister's not scared," they tell him.
I am petrified!
Lightning kills people.

I am tired of pushing his swing.
"Higher!" he yells. "Higher!"
"You learn to pump," I say.
"I like you pushing me," he says.

I am sick of doing up his seatbelt.
I hate having to praise his scribble pictures.

I'm sick of having a bath in water he's used first.
He leaves toys hidden under the last of the bubbles.
They are sharp to sit on and a bother to take out.
When I'm halfway through, he jumps out of bed
And runs in to whisper, "I peed in there."

Mama laughs.
"No, you didn't," she says.
But what does she know? He is sneaky.

I'm sick of his roaring I've hit him
When I barely touched him.
"Poor baby," they say — and kiss the spot.
What spot?
When he hammers me and I tell,
"Don't be a tattletale," they say.
Nobody believes me, let alone kisses the bruise,
Which can be seen clearly if anyone was interested.

I am tired of watching him curl up on their laps
And suck his thumb.
I could still fit,
But they laugh and push me off.
"You are a big girl now," they tell me.
"Me big boy," he says around the thumb.
"Yes, you are," they say, hugging him.

Jean Little

I'm sick of being sent to tidy up his mess.
So maybe one tiny thing is mine,
But the other four hundred are his.
Why can't they see that?
"Don't argue about it; DO it," they snap.

They told me I would love
Having a little brother or sister.
Ha!

Get Lost

"Get lost!" I yelled at him.
He ran off, bawling.
I didn't care.
Let him tell.

Then I needed him to be the Bad Guy.
I could not find him anywhere.
Mom and Dad hadn't noticed he was missing.
He didn't show up until just before supper.

Sometimes you must lose something
Before you know you can't get along without it.

Grumps

I was seven when my mother had her gall bladder out.
I had to stay with her aunts.
Great Aunt Charlotte and Great Aunt Juliet.
They were old and they complained all the time.
Their joints hurt and they woke up stiff.
Every time they got out of a chair,
They grunted like giant hippos.
They fed me stuff like pork and beans out of a tin
And Kraft Dinner and rhubarb.
They made me cups of tea that were all milk and sugar.
They read their favorite books out loud to me,
But they fell asleep just when things got interesting.
They talked about going out
For a walk for the good of their health,
But they only did it twice. Huff, puff, wheeze.
Sometimes neither of them spoke a word for over an hour.
I can't remember them laughing.

They're dead now and I'm grown up.
But one moment of the visit stays clear in my mind.
They had been sniping at each other.
Aunt Charlotte had left the spoon in the jam
Instead of washing it.
Aunt Juliet had spilled tea over the phone book.
They got mad and stopped speaking and I hated it there.

Then Aunt Charlotte read the paper
And said, in a queer voice,
"Sally Buller is gone. In her seventy-third year."
The silence changed completely.
I stared at them, not knowing what had happened.

Then, out of the blue,
Aunt Juliet said, "I love you, Charlotte."
"Yes," said Aunt Charlotte in a shaky voice. "And I you."

For about six minutes, everything changed.
I thought the grumps were over.

Then Aunt Charlotte said, "You have jam on your dress."
And Aunt Juliet said,
"Personal remarks are not in good taste."
And they were off again.

Did they hate each other or love each other?
I only glimpsed the love that once.
But...I'm old enough now to know it was there.

Birth Places

My best friend ever since kindergarten
Is from Pakistan.
My second best friend just moved here
From Hong Kong.
The smartest kid in my class is Nigerian.
He can beat my father at chess.

Where am I from?
Don't ask. It is too boring.

Vancouver.

I was born in Toronto,
But that's no help.

I want to be from Timbuktu
Or Zanzibar.

Why didn't my parents think ahead?

Nadya's Cat

Nadya's cat Dancer
Is beautiful.
Nadya loves him
With all her heart.
The only times she doesn't
Are when she is picking up the corpses
Of mice and moles
And the bodies of little birds
Who have sung their last song.

Giving Dancer extra kibble does not help.
Scolding doesn't either.
Even Nadya's tears don't touch his heart.
He's proud of himself.
He waits for her to say "Clever cat."
Sometimes, right in front of her,
He even licks his whiskers.

I Gave My Mom a Castle

"What do you want for your birthday?"
We asked my mother.
Then Dad, Clara, Hank and I waited.
Mom looked dreamy.
"All I really want," she said slowly,
"Is a castle —
A castle devoid of clutter and free from chaos,
With servants to wait on me hand and foot."

Dad got her a painting of a castle.
They hung it over the fireplace.
"It's gorgeous," she said.

Hank wrote her a story about a queen
Who lived in a castle.
He illustrated it himself.
It was three pages long.
She sat right down and read it with his help.
His printing is wobbly and his spelling baffles us.
"Hank, you are a genius," she said.

Clara bought her a tiny castle
To hang on her charm bracelet.
After she finally found the bracelet,
She smiled at the tiny castle dangling from her wrist.
"What a clever daughter!" she said.

I got staples and filled her personal stapler.
I got a big roll of Scotch tape for her empty dispenser.
I hung paper towels where they are supposed to go
And put toilet paper rolls in all the holders.
I got a large box of Kleenex for each bathroom.

I even opened them and pulled out the top tissue.
I vacuumed the downstairs.
I figured castle bedrooms were probably left to chance.
I ran a couple of loads of laundry
Through the washer and dryer.
I even folded the clean clothes.
I emptied the dishwasher and put the stuff away.
She hates emptying it.

Then I biked to the florist's shop
And bought her a rose.
I'd have picked her wildflowers
But there aren't any in January.
Even one rose was not cheap.

All the same, the whole thing only cost me
A week's allowance and a weekend's time.

She went all around, noticing things.
Then she said, "Thank you, Jim,
For making my wish come true."

"But, Mother," Clara protested,
"You wished for a castle.
Jim didn't give you a castle at all."

"When you are my age, Clara," my mother said,
"And you long for a castle,
May God give you a son like Jim."

Sticks and Stones

When my dad was a kid,
He got picked on.
"Laugh it off," his dad told him.
"Sticks and stones may break your bones,
But names will never hurt you," his mother said.
He couldn't laugh.
The names did hurt.
Once in awhile there were sticks and stones too.

Barney Hutton and his friends began picking on me.
I wear thick glasses.
My name is Mortimer after my grandad.
And I'm small — so far,
A lot smaller than Barney.
I also wear one hearing aid.
"Shortie Mortie," he calls me.
And other names.
"Tin ear."

My dad went to the school to complain.
Miss Weller, my teacher,
Told him children were more thoughtful now.
"I've never once seen anyone
Pick on Mortimer," she told him.

My dad looked at her.
Then he said, very quietly,
"Nobody picked on me either —
When the teacher was looking."

My dad is really tall.
The teacher looked up to him.

"I can talk to the principal," she said.
"But it isn't happening on school property."

Dad went to see Barney's folks.
They said Barney wouldn't pick on anybody.
But they must have yelled at him after Dad left.
Things are slightly better.

Sticks and stones and names still hurt.
And laughing isn't such a great shield.
What I really want is somebody on my side.
What I need is a big friend.

Season's Tickets

My big sister Barbara is bats about baseball.
When my father gave me *Touching All The Bases*
By Claire Mackay for Christmas,
I read bits of it.
It was pretty good.
It made me laugh.
But Barbara memorized it.
Just ask her.
She knows every single baseball fact in that book
And lots Claire Mackay didn't put in.

Yet when Dad got two season's tickets to the Dome,
He meant me to go with him.
Taking Barbara never crossed his mind.

Well, baseball's okay,
But I don't want to waste all my summer weekends
Watching the Jays
Run around on those miles of Astroturf.

I want to be a scientist.
I want to learn all I can
About turtles and toads and snakes.
I like reading books about them, but
I want to observe them too.
I like being outside in swamps or beside creeks.
I lie on my stomach and watch them for hours.
I don't care how many mosquitoes bite me.

I tried to tell Dad, but he refused to listen.

Barbara's twelfth birthday is on May 22.

I bought a card.
"This card entitles you to take my place
At all the baseball games
Dad is going to this summer," I wrote.
"Happy birthday."

Dad was miffed.
He hardly spoke to me for about a week.
But the first time he took Barbara,
They had such a great time
That I don't think he'll want to take me ever again.

She knows everybody's batting average,
Which team they used to play for,
What pitches they shouldn't try.

Before they are out of the driveway,
Mom smiles at me and picks up her book.
I smile back and head for the nearest toad terrain.

It was the best present I ever gave anybody.
The cheapest too.

Sundial

My mother got a sundial for our garden.
It says, "I count only the sunny hours."
But when I was out there on the night of Canada Day,
I ran over to it with my sparkler.
It got to count a sparkling minute.
I'll bet it counts moony hours too sometimes,
But my mom won't let me stay up long enough to check.

I Am Very Quiet

I am very quiet. Everybody says so.
I am very shy. They say that too.
But one of these days
I'm planning to surprise them.
I'll wear hot pink and raise a hullabaloo.

Will they take me to a therapist,
   Tell me to behave myself,
      Pretend it isn't happening
         Or hug me and yell "Yahoo!"?

I wish I knew.

The Table Said

"He ran slam into me," the table said.
"Whacked his little bullet head into my bad leg.
Then he shouted, 'Table hit me!'
And he slapped me as hard as he could.
I know he's only two, but it really stung.
'Bad table,' he said.

I'm thinking of suing.
The dining room chairs were all witnesses.
They are dependable.
They are oak."

"You are ridiculous,"
The plastic chair in the corner said.
"Nobody will take you seriously.
You're nothing but an old table."

"What does she know?
She's only six months old
And she came from Canadian Tire.

I am oak, like the chairs,
And I belonged to the child's
Great great-grandfather.
I am one hundred and two.
I was a wedding present from his bride's family.
If they took me to the Antique Road Show, they would
find out what a treasure I am.

The child just crawled underneath me
And found my secret shelf.
'Ooo,' he said.

Then he trotted off and got his two prize chestnuts.
And he hid them there.
'Good old table,' he said.

His great-grandfather hid things there
And his grandmother.

Maybe I'll wait.
He might turn out all right yet.
I'll give him the benefit of the doubt,"
the table said.

Miss Sorenson and Mother's Day

Miss Sorenson had had the children in her third grade class
Making Mother's Day cards every May
For twenty-six years.

She knew that, these days, some of them had a problem,
But she was thoughtful.
"Write 'For My Special Person,'" she told them.
"Or you can just put 'My Aunt' or 'My Grandma.'
I know there's someone
Who will be happy to get your card on Sunday."

Dylan was a special case, though.
He was in his third foster home and he was just nine.
When she made her little speech,
He stared at her with hard, angry eyes.

"Have you a problem, dear?" she asked him.
She did not think, until later, that everyone was listening.

"I don't want to make one," he growled.
"I'll draw an airplane."

She could not let him get away with that.
He always drew planes with bombs falling out of them.
She put her hand on his shoulder
And gave him her best smile.
"No, that is not the idea.
You have to make a card for someone.
Your foster mother would be thrilled, I know.
Try your best, Dylan.
If you don't want to make it for your foster mother,
How about your baby-sitter?

There must be someone who is special to you," she said.
Then she moved on.
She did not know why, but she wanted to run.
Of course, she did no such thing.

She watched, from the corner of her eye, and saw him
Working away.
He was shoving down hard on his marker.
But he crammed the card into the envelope provided
And left with it in his backpack.

She was late leaving.
At first, seeing from a distance that something
Had been slipped under her windshield wiper,
She thought it was an advertisement.

Then she drew closer and saw Dylan's envelope.
Was he saying she was special?
She knew she did not believe that.
She wasn't.
She didn't even like him really.
She pulled the envelope free
And drove all the way home before she opened it.

Jean Little

All that was inside was a picture of a woman,
An extremely ugly woman,
Crying fat tears and talking on a big black telephone.
"I will think of you, darling, every Mother's Day,"
Said the balloon coming out of her mouth.

On a separate piece of paper,
In big, black letters, was written,
"You deliver it, teacher.
I don't know where she is."

The teacher stared down at what she held.
She knew, without any doubt,
That the woman was Dylan's mother.
Nobody knew where she had gone.

Should she take it straight to the school psychologist?
Or the principal...

She went to bed early and cried tears of her own.
What made it so terrible was the small arrow
Next to the tears.
And the one word FAKE.

On Monday, she walked up to the boy.
"I couldn't do it," she told him, looking straight at him.
"I am sorry, Dylan.
I don't know how to find her."

"Who cares where she is," he whispered.

But she thought she saw the tension ease ever so slightly
In his thin shoulders.

And on the Friday before Father's Day,
She took her class on a field trip to the arboretum.

Bad Guys

"I'm tired of telling Batman stories,"
I told my little brother.
"Just this once can I tell you 'The Three Little Pigs'?"

"No," he snapped.
"There's no bad guys in it.
I like bad guys."

So much for you, Big Bad Wolf.

Dead Worm

My little sister, Melissa Joan, found a worm.
She pinched it until it came apart in the middle.
Then she toddled up to my brother Luke and held it out.
"Eeeek! Get that away from me!" Luke yelled.

Melissa looked surprised, but she turned away.
Holding out the oozing worm halves, still wiggling,
She started for Mother.
"Outside," Mother said in a kind of roar.
"Take it outside, sweetheart, and let it GO!
March, Melissa Joan Bagshaw, this instant!"

Then Melissa brought her two-piece worm to me.

"Thank you," I said and took both of it.
When she went looking for more,
I tossed it in the garbage.
Then I got the wagon and pulled her
Up and down the driveway rapidly
To get her mind off worms.

Good manners are important to a baby.
I'm only six.
I remember.
Mother and Luke didn't like slugs either.

"What's Christmas, Ben?"

Ben was the youngest child.

"Do you remember Christmas, Ben?"
Asked his big sister Jeanie.

"Maybe," said Ben.

"Christmas is an evergreen tree,"
Jeanie told him,
"With lights and tinsel and a star."

"Star on top," said Ben.

"Christmas is secrets," said Katie.
"Wrapping presents and hiding them
In a safe place."

"Shhh. Don't tell," said Ben.

"Christmas is turkey and mince pie," said Gram,
"And second helpings all around."

"Candy canes," yelled Ben,
"And gingerbread boys."

"Christmas is going carol singing
After supper," said Emilie dreamily,
"Seeing the stars and sounding like angels."

"Jingle bells, jingle bells," sang Ben.

"Christmas is hanging up my stocking for Santa.
He comes down the chimney
With toys for me," said Daniel firmly.

"Ho, ho, ho!" roared Ben.

"Christmas is special books to share," said Aunt Jean,
"And stories to tell by the fire."

"Humbug!" said Ben.

"He does remember," cried Jeanie.
"What's Christmas, Ben?"

"Christmas is a baby," said Ben softly.
"A baby
Just like me."

The Dish

I was seven, I think, or maybe eight
When I gave my mother the flowered dish.
I knew she loved buying bowls and platters
with patterns of fruit or flowers on them.
She would choose them so carefully
And I would have to wait another week
For new gym shoes.
She ignored notes from my teacher.

So, when her birthday neared,
I thought I knew what she'd like.
I went to the gift shop and bought
A small oval dish with roses on it.
It cost more than I owned, but
I borrowed the rest from Dad.

"That's lovely, darling," she said,
Turning it over to read what was written underneath.
I looked later.
It said "Bone China, Made in England."

She left it on the table that evening,
But the next day it vanished.
She came home with a new dish,
Much the same size.
It said "Royal Doulton" on the bottom.

That afternoon I saw the dish I'd bought her.
It was back in the shop.
I took it to the man behind the counter.
"This is just like the one I bought my mother," I said.

"Oh, yes," he said, glancing at it.
"She traded it in on a nice bit of Royal Doulton.
She has a real eye for precious things."

I am forty-three now and my mother is dead.
Yet it still hurts me
That she wanted a Royal Doulton child,
But I was only bone china.

Why My Aunt Miranda is Not Married

"Why didn't you get married?" I asked my Aunt Miranda.
"Marriage was the one mistake I didn't make," she said.
"But didn't you want children?" I asked,
Not looking straight at her.
"I wanted a child like a library book," she said.
"Like a library book! What kind of kid is that?"
I said, after waiting a long minute.
"One I can borrow and return, of course," she told me.
I was growing angry when she added,
"You I keep renewing.
There is nothing in this world that I love more
Than a great library book."

I was mad, but only for a moment.
After all, I know what she means.
There's nothing I love more than a good library book,
And when I find a practically perfect one,
I take it out over and over.

Aunt Miranda has been borrowing me regularly
Ever since I can remember.

Names

We have a Sunbeam in our class.
We have an Apple too.
My sister knows a Dimples
And I've a friend called Blue.

There's a boy in Grade Eight
Named November.
There's a Stormy in Grade Seven.
There's Cherub and there's Harmony
And Juniper and Heaven.

I like names that aren't usual.
I think it's great they vary.
But I'm glad my mother kept her head
And called me Mary.

Maudie Alone

Maudie wore a key around her neck.
"You'll never need it.
Someone will always be here to let you in.
But just in case," her mother said.

Maudie almost forgot about her key.
Until, one Tuesday afternoon in December,
It happened.
Nobody was home.
Maudie knocked and waited and knocked again.
Nobody.
Then Maudie fitted the key into the keyhole
And turned it slowly.
The lock clicked open.
She stepped forward into her quiet, empty house.
For the first time in her life,
She was all on her own.

She stood in the hall and listened.
The grandfather clock ticked loudly.
"Hi, hi! Hi, hi!" it said.
"Hi, Grandfather," Maudie whispered with a small smile.
He had never spoken to her before.

A shadowy little girl in a tall mirror gazed at her.
Maudie waved.
The mirror girl waved back.

Maudie raised one hand above her head.
She pointed her toe.
Slowly she spun around.
Then, coming back to the beginning,

She swept a low curtsy.
She only wobbled a tiny bit coming up.

"I am Natasha," she said in a high voice.
"They are begging me for one more encore,
But my heart is broken.
How can I dance with a broken heart?"

Then she ran away from the mirror
To the top of the long staircase.
Quickly, quickly, she flung one leg over the banister
And whizzed down.
She raced back up and did it again.
Three times.
Perfectly.
Flying fast.
Free.
Against the rules.

She was at the bottom when she heard the garage door.
Spry as Jack Be Nimble, she leapt off the stairs,
Sped into the living room
And pushed the button on the big TV.

She sat down on the couch.
She arranged her face.
Bored, a little tired, pleased someone was home.

"Maudie, sweetheart," called her mother.
"I'm so sorry.
There was construction and the doctor kept me late.
Were you frightened?"

"No," said Maudie calmly, watching the screen.
"It was okay.
I used my key."

She reached up and touched the key softly.
There would be other times.
Someday she would get to turn the key again
And find herself waiting.
Her all-alone self,
The secret Maudie inside.
Maudie alone.
She and her key would wait.